# DUKE
# DUKE 2000
## WHATEVER IT TAKES 2000

## Recent Doonesbury Books by G.B. Trudeau

Read My Lips, Make My Day, Eat Quiche and Die!
Give Those Nymphs Some Hooters!
You're Smokin' Now, Mr. Butts!
I'd Go With the Helmet, Ray
Welcome to Club Scud!
What Is It, Tink, Is Pan in Trouble?
Quality Time on Highway 1
Washed Out Bridges and Other Disasters
In Search of Cigarette Holder Man
Doonesbury Nation
Virtual Doonesbury
Planet Doonesbury
Buck Wild Doonesbury

## Special Collections

The Doonesbury Chronicles
Doonesbury's Greatest Hits
The People's Doonesbury
Doonesbury Dossier:  The Reagan Years
Doonesbury Deluxe:  Selected Glances Askance
Recycled Doonesbury:  Second Thoughts on a Gilded Age
Action Figure!
The Portable Doonesbury
Flashbacks:  Twenty-Five Years of Doonesbury
The Bundled Doonesbury

A DOONESBURY BOOK

# DUKE DUKE 2000 2000
## WHATEVER IT TAKES

BY G. B. TRUDEAU

Andrews McMeel
Publishing

Kansas City

**DOONESBURY** is distributed internationally by Universal Press Syndicate.

*Duke 2000: Whatever It Takes* copyright © 2000 by G.B. Trudeau. All rights reserved. Printed in the United States of America. No part of this book may be used or reproduced in any manner whatsoever without written permission except in the case of reprints in the context of reviews. For information, write Andrews McMeel Publishing, an Andrews McMeel Universal company, 4520 Main Street, Kansas City, Missouri 64111.

00 01 02 03 04  BAM  10 9 8 7 6 5 4 3 2 1

ISBN: 0-7407-0607-1

Library of Congress Catalog Card Number: 00-103485

**DOONESBURY** may be viewed on the Internet at:
www.doonesbury.com and www.uexpress.com

**ATTENTION: SCHOOLS AND BUSINESSES**

Andrews McMeel books are available at quantity discounts with bulk purchase for educational, business, or sales promotional use. For information, please write to: Special Sales Department, Andrews McMeel Publishing, 4520 Main Street, Kansas City, Missouri 64111.

"I understand small business growth. I was one."

—George W. Bush

TERRY! TALK TO ME! MAKE ME HAPPY YOU CALLED!

NO CAN DO, BABE...

THE STUDIO JUST DECIDED TO POSTPONE YOUR CLIENT'S SPLATTER FLICK, FOR A WEEK OR SO. YOU KNOW, OUT OF RESPECT FOR LITTLETON...

RIGHT THING TO DO, BABE. BEAUTIFUL GESTURE. I'M MOVED.

YOU ARE?

YOU KIDDING? I'M PRACTICALLY BAWLING HERE! A WEEK, YOU SAY?

TOPS, NO WAY THIS TRAGEDY HAS LEGS.

OLLIE! SID HERE! BAD NEWS, BABE — THE STUDIO'S REPOSITIONING THE OPENING OF "SPLATTERED"!

YOU MEAN, OVER THE COLUMBINE THING. WHAT'S UP WITH THAT? THEY MUST HAVE TEN HIGH SCHOOL REVENGE FILMS LINED UP! WHY MINE?

HEY...OLLIE! WILL YOU LISTEN TO YOURSELF HERE? SHOW A LITTLE CLASS, OKAY?

⋛SIGH⋛... HOW LONG?

TWO WEEKS, MAX. LUCAS OWNS JUNE ANYWAY.

TERRY? SID. I TALKED TO MY CLIENT ABOUT POSTPONING HIS FILM...

HE'S A LITTLE STEAMED, AND I CAN'T BLAME HIM. I MEAN, YOU'RE OPENING "KILLER CLIQUE" THE SAME WEEKEND!

THAT ONE'S GOT SEVEN CHEERLEADER MURDERS, A TEACHER BEHEADING AND SEVERAL RAPES. WHAT'S THE DIFFERENCE?

IT'S A SATIRE.

OH, RIGHT. THE SEND-UP THING.

FINALLY, TONIGHT WE BID ADIEU TO AN OLD COLLEAGUE.

ROLAND BURTON HEDLEY JR. HAS WORKED HERE AT ABC WIDE WORLD OF NEWS FOR OVER 20 YEARS.

TODAY HE LEAVES FOR THE LUSHER PASTURES OF THE INTERNET, JOINING YAP.COM AS CHIEF CONTENT PROVIDER. WE WISH HIM ALL THE BEST.

"CHIEF CONTENT PROVIDER"?

GOOD EVENING.

FOR THE YAP NETWORK, THIS IS CHIEF CONTENT PROVIDER **ROLAND HEDLEY** WITH A LIVE WEBCAST FROM A GEORGE W. BUSH PRESS AVAILABILITY!

TODAY GOV. BUSH ONCE AGAIN DESCRIBED HIMSELF AS A "COMPASSIONATE CONSERVATIVE," THUS DEMONSTRATING A STRONG COMMITMENT TO HAVING IT BOTH WAYS.

THERE'S MORE, BUT IT WOULD MEAN A PROHIBITIVE DOWNLOAD TIME. I'M ROLAND HEDLEY.

WHO'S THE TEENY LITTLE MAN, POPPY?

HE'S A CHIEF CONTENT PROVIDER.

THIS IS **ROLAND HEDLEY** NARROWCASTING LIVE FROM A GEORGE W. BUSH PRESS AVAILABILITY!

AND I INTEND TO BE A **COMPASSIONATE** CONSERVATIVE!

GOVERNOR, IF "CONSERVATIVE" HAS TO BE MODIFIED BY THE WORD "COMPASSIONATE," ISN'T THAT AN ADMISSION THAT CONSERVATISM IS NOT INHERENTLY A GENEROUS PHILOSOPHY?

ISN'T IT A BIT LIKE BEING A "BENIGN DESPOT" OR AN "HONEST THIEF" OR A "SOCIAL DRINKER"?

UM, NOT AT ALL....

GOVERNOR, SPEAKING OF SOCIAL DRINKING...

I WON'T PLAY GOTCHA. WON'T DO IT. NOT MY BAG.

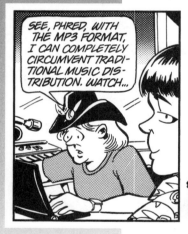

AL, WALK ME THROUGH A TYPICAL SPEECH. MAYBE I CAN HELP OUT HERE.

WELL, I ALWAYS OPEN WITH A COUPLE OF JOKES — AT MY *OWN* EXPENSE, I MIGHT ADD — JOKES ABOUT MY STIFFNESS, ETC.

THEN I SEGUE INTO ONE OF MY BIG ISSUES, LIKE SUBURBAN SPRAWL...

SUBURBAN SPRAWL?

CORRECT. LET ME EXPLAIN...

ZZZ,

AL, THERE ARE A LOT OF STRATEGIES YOU COULD BE USING TO OVERCOME YOUR DULLNESS PROBLEM...

FOR INSTANCE, NEVER UNDERESTIMATE THE IMPACT OF A WELL-PLACED LIE...

DO YOU KNOW THAT I ONCE DELIVERED A SPEECH IN WHICH I TOLD NO LESS THAN 57 DISTINCT LIES?

WOW... *REALLY?*

NO. BUT SEE HOW I GOT YOUR ATTENTION?

AL, LET'S JUST ADMIT WHAT THE PROBLEM IS HERE — YOU'RE A VICTIM OF MY SUCCESS.

THE COUNTRY'S ON CRUISE CONTROL, AND SO VOTERS REALLY DON'T FEEL THE NEED TO SHOP FOR QUALIFICATIONS ANYMORE...

THEY FEEL SAFE TO CHOOSE SOME EASYGOING HUCKLEBERRY WITH A CROOKED GRIN, A BOYISH TWINKLE, AND A LOVE FOR MIXING IT UP WITH EVERYDAY FOLK. HEAR WHAT I'M SAYING, AL?

YES. YOU'RE SAYING I SHOULD JUST BE MYSELF.

LET ME TRY AGAIN...

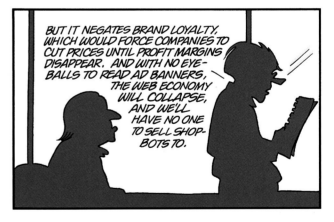

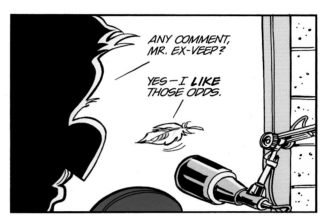

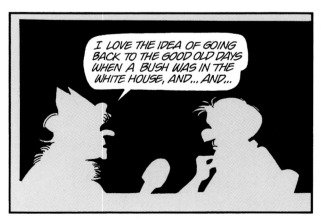

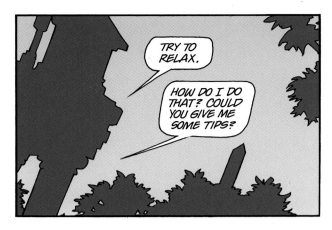

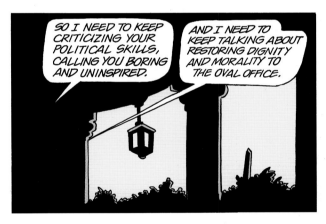

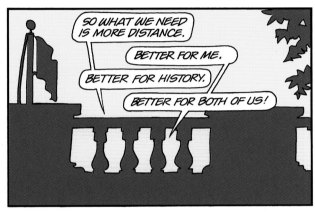

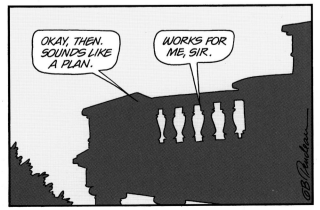

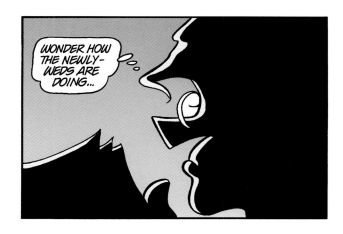

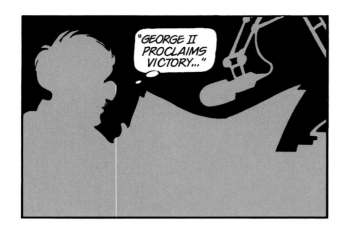

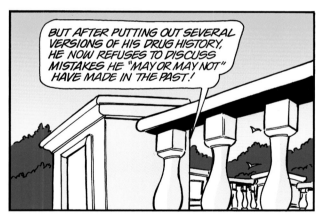

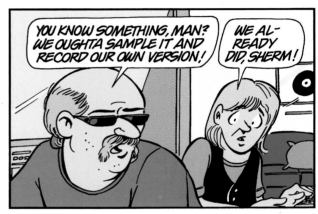

GOVERNOR BUSH, PEOPLE SEEM A LITTLE WORRIED THAT YOU'VE NEVER DONE MUCH WITHOUT THE BENEFIT OF CONNECTIONS...

EVEN YOUR "POSITIONS" SEEM TO HAVE BEEN PROVIDED FOR YOU LIKE PURCHASED TERM PAPERS.

TO USE AN OLD TEXAS PHRASE, AREN'T YOU "ALL HAT AND NO CATTLE"?

DEFINE "CATTLE."

AS IN "WHERE'S THE BEEF?"

NOT FOLLOWING YOU. NEXT QUESTION.

BEEF? YOU WANT BEEF, ELITE MEDIA GUY! COMIN' ATCHA ON A PLATTER!

TAKE MY NEW PROPOSALS FOR HEAD START! IF THAT'S NOT BEEF, I DON'T KNOW WHAT IS!

ACTUALLY, SIR, IT'S NOT CLEAR WHAT YOU'RE GOING FOR HERE...

LET ME SEE IF I'VE GOT IT STRAIGHT — YOU'RE CAMPAIGNING FOR THE GOP NOMINATION ON A PROMISE TO FINE-TUNE A CLASSIC DEMOCRATIC SOCIAL PROGRAM?

UH...YES. BUT ONLY UNTIL WE CAN KILL IT.

DOH! OF COURSE — THE TAX CUT!

GOVERNOR BUSH, YOU RECENTLY SEEMED TO IMPLY THAT YOU USED COCAINE BEFORE 1975, THAT IS, BEFORE IT WAS COMMONLY USED IN SOCIAL CIRCLES LIKE YOURS...

DO YOU REALLY EXPECT THE AMERICAN PEOPLE TO BELIEVE YOU WERE THAT CUTTING EDGE IN YOUR CHOICE OF STREET DRUGS?

NO! I MEAN YES! I...

LOOK! I'LL TALK ABOUT MY SEX LIFE! I'LL TALK ABOUT MY ALCOHOL ABUSE! BUT I WILL NOT DISCUSS SOMETHING AS PERSONAL AND PRIVATE AS COCAINE!

GOVERNOR, IS IT TRUE YOU ONCE DATED NIXON'S DAUGHTER?

OUT OF PATRIOTISM. I WAS IN THE GUARD THEN.

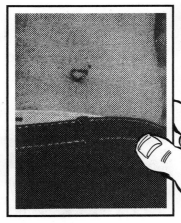

SURE, THIS MAY SEEM LIKE "DISTANT PAST" TERRITORY TO SOME PEOPLE...

BUT IN A CIVILIZED SOCIETY, PEOPLE AREN'T BRANDED WITH LITTLE DELTAS TO PROVE THEIR ALLEGIANCE TO A FRATERNAL ORDER!

THE FACT IS GEORGE BUSH ONCE PRESIDED OVER SAVAGE INITIATION RITES THAT INCLUDED BEATINGS AND THE SEARING OF HUMAN FLESH!

BUT WASN'T THAT ALL PART OF THE FUN?

IT WAS IN MY DAY!

IF I HAVE TO GO IT ALONE, I WILL!

I GOTTA ASK HIM! MY YAP.COM AUDIENCE DESERVES HARD ANSWERS!

YOU DO WHAT YOU HAVE TO, ROLAND...

GOVERNOR?

YES?

SIR, DO YOU STILL SUPPORT FRATERNAL MUTILATION RITES?

UM...

DISTANT PAST! DISTANT PAST!

WELL, LOOKS LIKE YOU SCARED HIM OFF, ROLLIE...

THAT'S IT, GOVERNOR, BE AFRAID. BE VERY AFRAID!

YOU CAN'T AVOID THE TOUGH QUESTIONS FOREVER! WHEREVER YOU GO, YAP.COM WILL BE THERE, TOO, DEMANDING THE TRUTH!

POOR GUY. I ALMOST FEEL SORRY FOR HIM...

DON'T! IF HE WANTS TO RUN WITH THE BIG DOGS, HE'S GOT TO BE ABLE TO HANDLE HARD-NOSED REPORTING!

QUITE RIGHT!

WELL, OFF TO GRILL MRS. DOLE ABOUT VIAGRA!

HAPPY HUNTING!

64

MIKE, HOW COME YOU'RE SUPPORTING McCAIN INSTEAD OF FORBES AGAIN?

I DUNNO, I GUESS I JUST ADMIRE HIM MORE. HE SEEMS TO BE THE ONLY ONE OUT THERE WHO'S HOLDING ON TO HIS DIGNITY...

WHICH AIN'T EASY IN A FIELD THAT INCLUDES DONALD TRUMP, JESSE VENTURA, PAT BUCHANAN, WARREN BEATTY, AND GOD KNOWS WHO ELSE.

WHY NOT, SIR? EVERY **OTHER** CARTOON CHARACTER IS RUNNING!

HOW MUCH DOES IT PAY AGAIN?

SIR, I'VE GIVEN THIS A LOT OF THOUGHT—THIS IS YOUR YEAR! YOU COULD GO ALL THE WAY!

THE ONLY SERIOUS COMPETITION YOU'D FACE IS PAT BUCHANAN, AND HE'S A BIGOTED, MISOGYNIST, GAY-BASHING, ISOLATIONIST BROWNSHIRT!

BUCHANAN'S A BIGOTED, MISOGYNIST, GAY-BASHING, ISOLATIONIST BROWNSHIRT?

PRETTY MUCH.

SO WHAT THE HELL AM I SUPPOSED TO RUN ON?

THERE'S SOME OVERLAP, IT'S TRUE.

THE POINT IS, SIR, THE BAR HAS NEVER BEEN LOWER! IT'S NOT ABOUT CREDENTIALING ANYMORE— IT'S ABOUT BRANDING!

BESIDES, JESSE NEEDS A CANDIDATE FOR THE REFORM PARTY NOMINATION, AND ALL HE'S GOT NOW IS TRUMP!

TRUMP IS RUNNING? **DONALD** TRUMP?

YES, SIR.

WHAT JOB IS THIS AGAIN?

PRESIDENT. DON'T LET THE CANDIDATES THROW YOU.

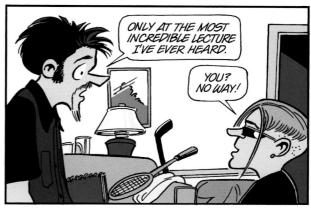

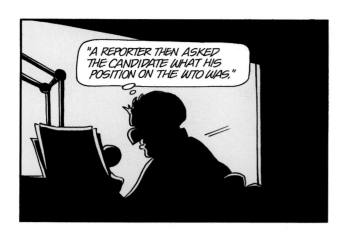

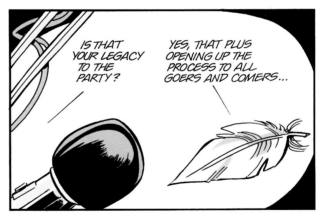

91

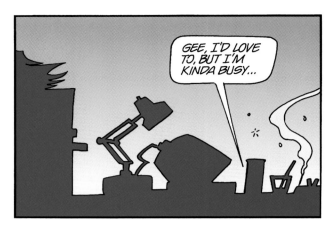

CAN YOU BELIEVE THIS, HONEY? **NO ONE** OFFERS LONG-TERM ESCORT LEASES! IT'S ALL BY THE HOUR! SOME SERVICE ECONOMY!

OF COURSE, HIRING SOME ORDINARY CLOCK-PUNCHER MIGHT RESONATE WITH WORKING-CLASS VOTERS...

NO...NO, BETTER TO GO THE GLAMOUR ROUTE! I SHOULD BE DATING SOME FRESH, NEW FACE FROM THE ADULT FILM INDUSTRY, SAY!

SIR, THIS TIME I'M REALLY, REALLY, REALLY QUITTING.

OKAY, FINE, BUT I'M STILL WAITING FOR MY ICE.

YOU'RE RUNNING FOR WHAT, DUKE?

PRESIDENT...

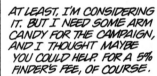

AT LEAST, I'M CONSIDERING IT. BUT I NEED SOME ARM CANDY FOR THE CAMPAIGN, AND I THOUGHT MAYBE YOU COULD HELP. FOR A 5% FINDER'S FEE, OF COURSE.

ARE YOU KIDDING ME? ARE YOU **KIDDING** ME? YOU WANT ME TO FIND YOU AN **ESCORT**? I'M AN **AGENT**, DUKE, NOT SOME PIMP!

OKAY, 10%!

YOU STILL OWE ME. GIVE ME THE SPECS.

DUKE? SID. I'VE GOT SOME CANDIDATES. TELL ME WHAT YOU'RE LOOKING FOR.

WELL, TRUMP'S LITTLE COOKIE IS A BRUNETTE, SO I WANT A BLONDE UPGRADE, PLUS A KILLER BODY.

WELL, THAT NARROWS THE FIELD...

PLUS, I DON'T WANT SOMEONE WITH TOO MUCH SELF-ESTEEM. THE CAMPAIGN ISN'T ABOUT THEM.

HMM... THAT JUST LEAVES...

NAH... SHE'D NEVER DO IT.

I NEED A CHANGE.

TAKE A CLASS.

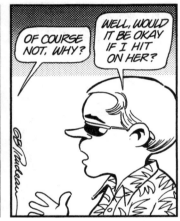

**O**N TO SOUTH CAROLINA.

SEN. McCAIN, ON THE SUBJECT OF FLYING THE CONFEDERATE FLAG, A SYMBOL OF RACISM TO MANY, YOU'VE SAID IT'S UP TO THE STATE.

FOR A GUY IDENTIFIED WITH INDEPENDENCE AND PERSONAL COURAGE, ISN'T YOUR REFUSAL TO TAKE A POSITION PRETTY COWARDLY?

WOW...TOUGH CHARGE, RICK! YOU'RE LUCKY I HAVE MY TEMPER UNDER CONTROL!

HA, HA, HA!

CHARMING.

UTTERLY.

LET'S GIVE HIM A PASS.

**D**UBYA'S TURN.

GOVERNOR, DO YOU AGREE WITH CRITICS WHO SAY SEN. McCAIN'S REFUSAL TO TAKE A STRONG STAND ON THE CONFEDERATE FLAG IS OUT OF CHARACTER?

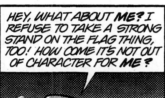

HEY, WHAT ABOUT **ME?** I REFUSE TO TAKE A STRONG STAND ON THE FLAG THING, TOO! HOW COME IT'S NOT OUT OF CHARACTER FOR **ME?**

WELL?

WE'RE TRYING TO KEEP IT A HORSE RACE, SIR.

ACTUALLY, I **DO** HAVE A STRONG STAND ON FLYING THE CONFEDERATE FLAG — IT'S UP TO THE PEOPLE OF SOUTH CAROLINA!

GOVERNOR, DO YOU THINK THAT OTHER SYMBOLS OF OFFICIAL RACISM, LIKE SEGREGATION AND DISCRIMINATION, SHOULD ALSO HAVE BEEN LEFT UP TO THE PEOPLE OF SOUTH CAROLINA?

UM...

SEARCHING... SEARCHING... E-4 ... NO, D-5!

JUST GIVE THE CHINESE A **WHIFF** OF FREEDOM!

CLOSE. IT'S D-7, SIR.

DUKE WEIGHS IN ON THE FLAG FLAP.

I'M A HEALER. WHAT I WOULD DO IS CUT THE TWO FLAGS IN TWO AND SEW TOGETHER A HALF FROM EACH! ANY QUESTIONS?

YES, WHAT ARE YOU DOING HERE? THIS IS THE REPUBLICAN PRIMARY. AREN'T YOU RUNNING ON THE REFORM PARTY TICKET?

I NEED TO BE BETTER PREPARED.

WE'RE A LITTLE SHORT-HANDED, SIR.

HONEY, WHAT AM I DOING IN SOUTH CAROLINA? I'M NOT A REPUBLICAN!

IT DOESN'T MATTER, SIR. WE HAVE TO GO WHERE THE FREE MEDIA ARE.

BUT ALL THEY WANT TO ASK ME ABOUT IS THAT DAMN FLAG!

IT'S AN IMPORTANT LOCAL ISSUE, SIR. YOU SHOULD HAVE A POSITION.

WHY? BOTH BUSH AND McCAIN HAVE DUCKED IT.

EXACTLY. YOU SHOULD BE THE ONE TO STAND UP TO THE RACISTS!

RACISTS? YOU MEAN PROUD HERITAGE BUFFS?

SIR, I DON'T HAVE **TIME** TO BUILD YOU A BACKBONE!

I THINK I'VE FIGURED OUT MY POSITION ON THE FLAG THING, HONEY. I WON'T CONDEMN IT AS A SYMBOL OF RACISM...

I'LL CONDEMN IT AS A SYMBOL OF LOSING! I MEAN, THEY LOST THE WAR! AND WHO DISPLAYS CONFEDERATE FLAGS TO THIS DAY? REDNECK **LOSERS!** THE STATE'S LOUSY WITH 'EM!

AND YOU'D BE REACHING OUT TO WHOM WITH THIS VIEW, SIR?

UM... I DUNNO... BLACKS?

BLACKS? YOU?

NO, THAT CAN'T BE RIGHT. WHO ELSE THEY GOT HERE?

SIR, IF WE DON'T COME UP WITH A FUND-RAISING STRATEGY SOON, THIS CAMPAIGN IS DEAD!

NOT TO WORRY. I'VE GOT AN IDEA...

SPONSORSHIPS! LIKE THE OLYMPICS! WE'LL GET CORPORATIONS TO **PAY** TO BE OFFICIAL SPONSORS OF THE DUKE 2000 CAMPAIGN. WHAT DO YOU THINK?

ASIDE FROM IT BEING ILLEGAL?

WHO'S GOING TO NOTICE? **NO ONE** UNDERSTANDS CAMPAIGN LAW ANYMORE!

WE COULD CALL IT REFORM, DAD!

THERE YOU GO. REFORM WITH RESULTS!

HOW ARE WE GOING TO GO ABOUT ATTRACTING SPONSORS, POP?

SIMPLE. WE PUT TOGETHER A DEMO REEL.

WE'LL USE IT TO PITCH CORPORATE AMERICA ON ALL THE ADVANTAGES OF PARTNERING WITH THE DUKE 2000 CAMPAIGN!

THIS IS SUCH A GREAT IDEA, DAD!

THANKS. YOU DON'T LOOK HAPPY, HONEY.

SIR, I'VE SEEN WHAT HAPPENS TO CHINESE FUND-RAISERS IN THIS COUNTRY.

HEY, YOU NEED TO FLEE, JUST COME SEE ME!

REFORM PARTY CANDIDATE DUKE HERE! YOU KNOW, GETTING YOUR MESSAGE OUT COSTS A LOT OF MONEY TODAY!

THAT'S WHY I HOPE TO BE IN TALKS WITH A FINE BEVERAGE COMPANY LIKE **LIPTON TEA** TO BE THE **OFFICIAL STIMULANT** OF THE DUKE 2000 CAMPAIGN!

TASTY LIPTON TEA— NOW **THAT'S** TEA! TRY SOME TODAY!

CUT! THAT'S A KEEPER! READY TO DO CHRYSLER?

THE MAKER OF FINE DRIVING MACHINES? YOU BET!

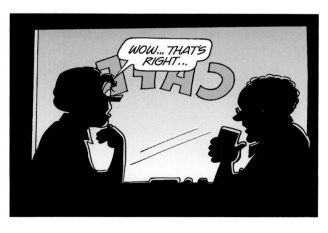

140

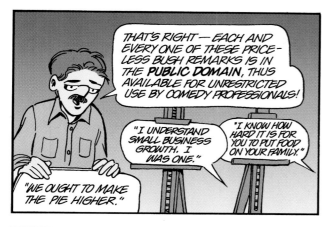